This book belongs to _____.

Color With Me!

Mom & Me
coloring Book

FALL

Sandy Mahony
Mary Lou Brown

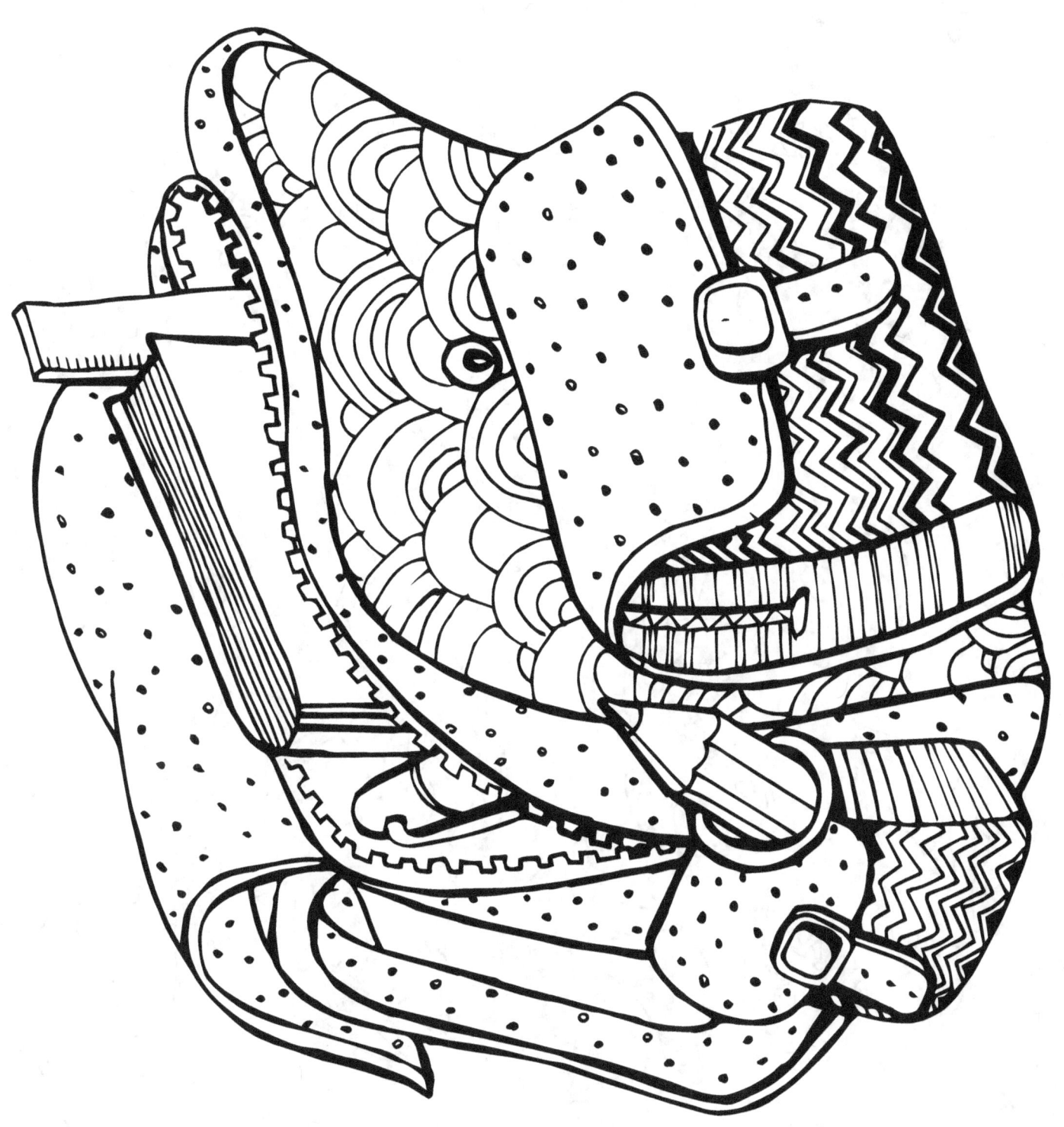

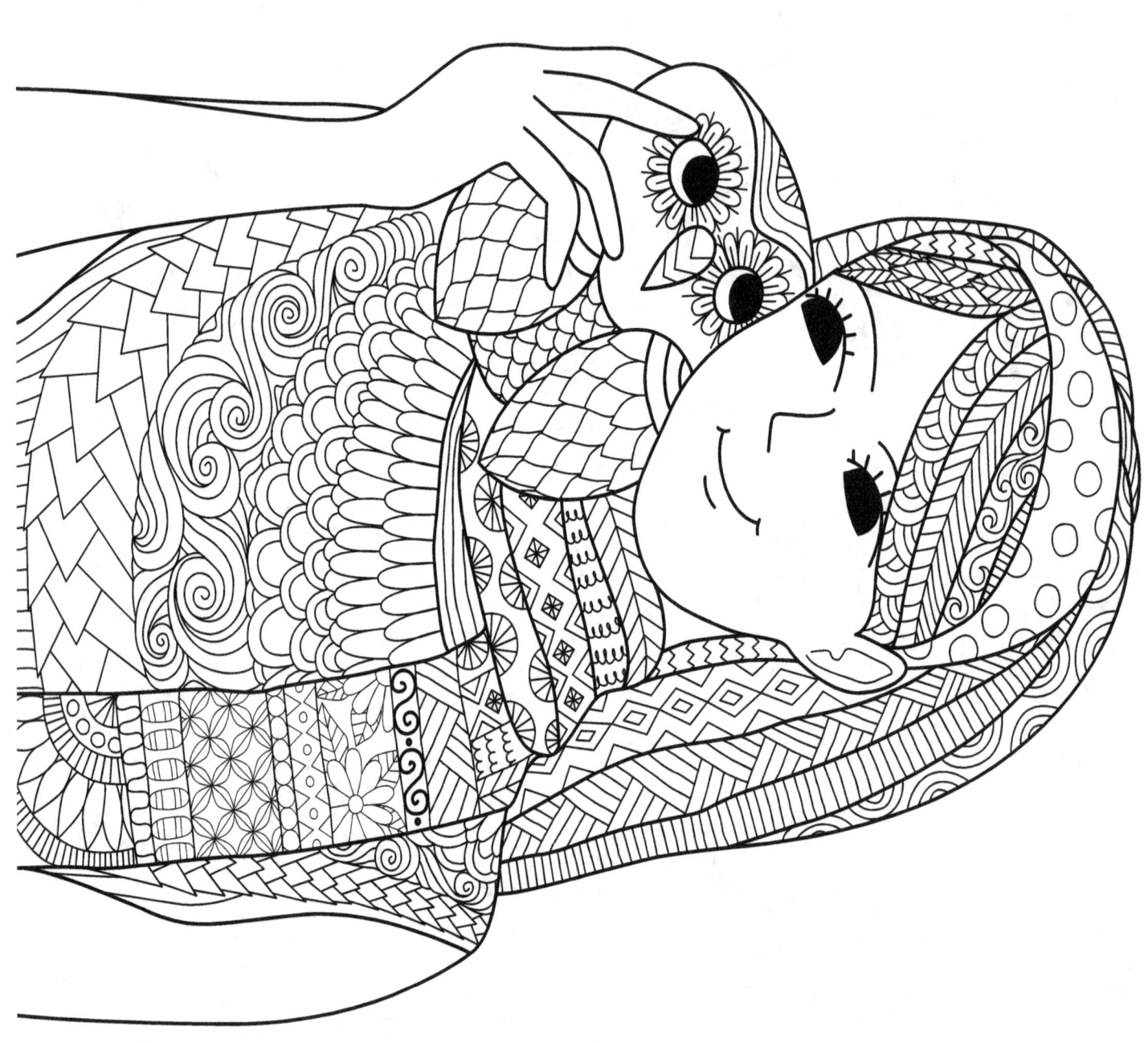

Autumn Season

jam

TRICK OR TREAT!

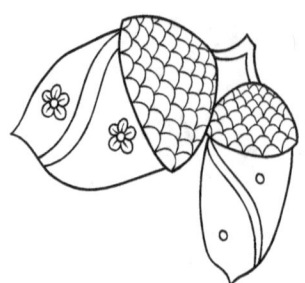

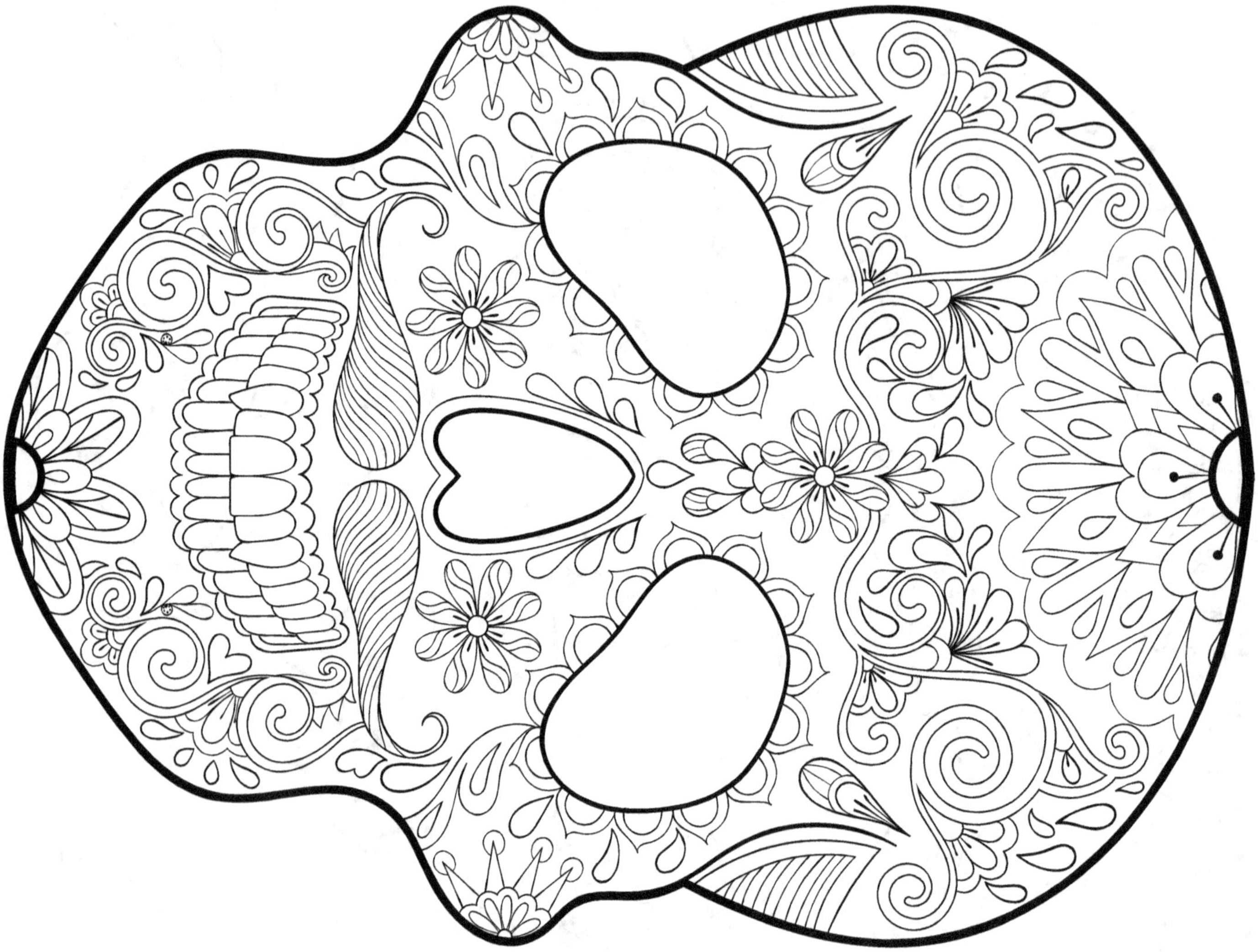

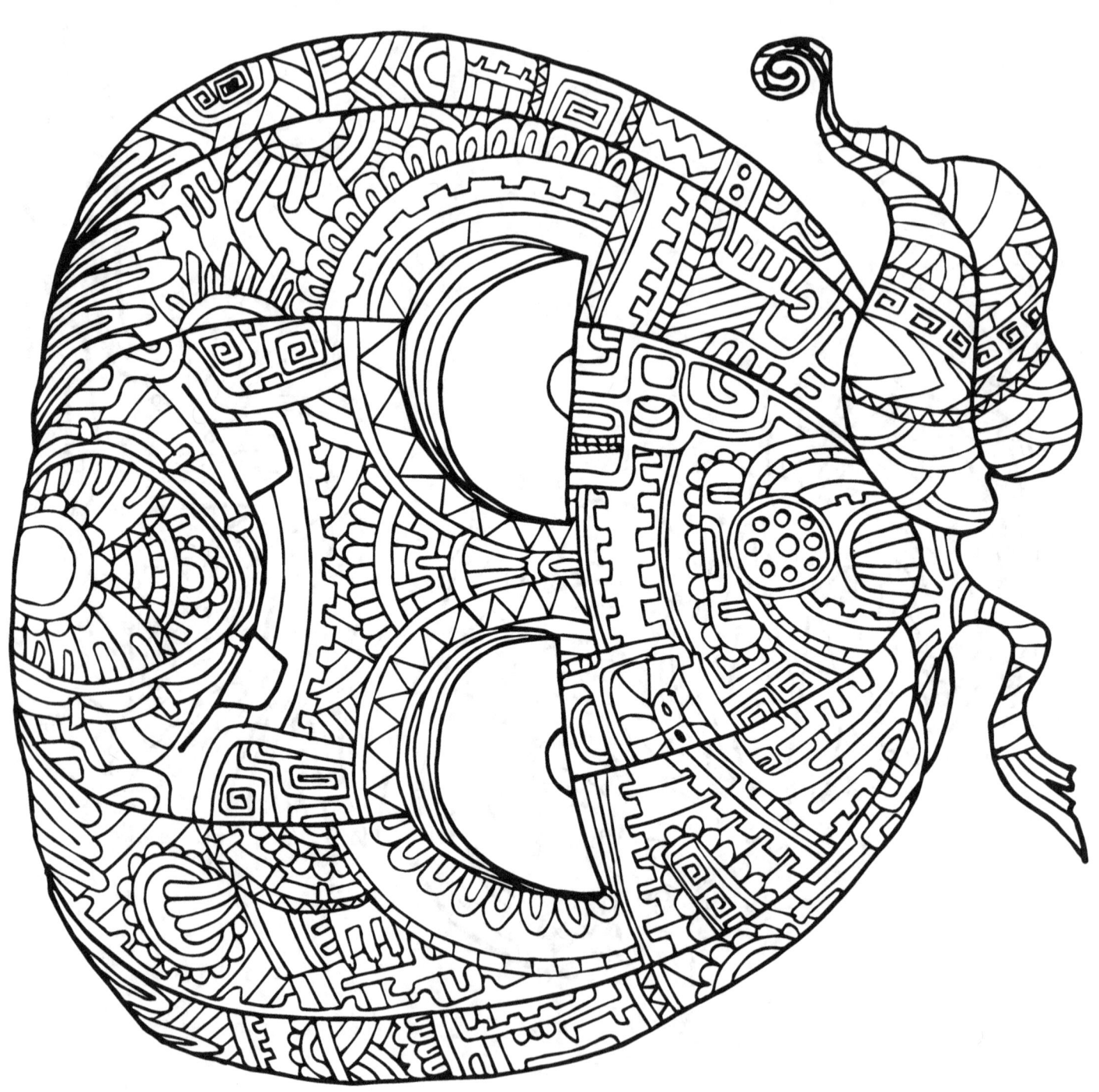

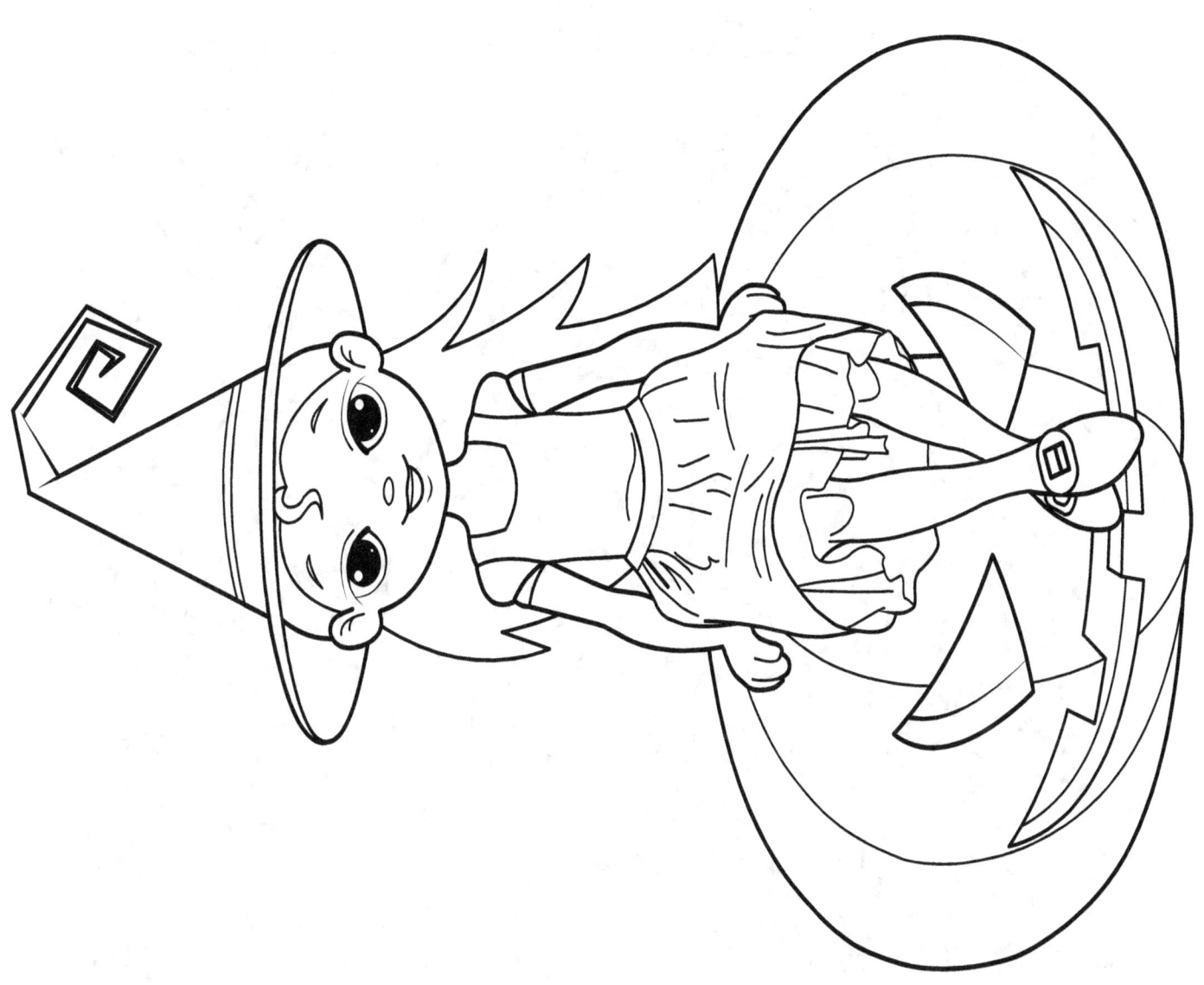

www.ingramcontent.com/pod-product-compliance
Lightning Source LLC
Chambersburg PA
CBHW081802280526
45789CB00008B/2958